In the Beginning

Based on Genesis 1:1-31

ISBN 0-687-09404-6

Text and illustrations copyright © 1996 Cokesbury.
Copyright © 2001 Abingdon Press
All rights reserved.

01 02 03 04 05 06 07 08 09 10—10 9 8 7 6 5 4 3 2 1

Abingdon Press • Nashville

Written by Judy Newman-St. John
Illustrated by Charles Jakubowski

In the beginning,
In the beginning,
God created the world,
   a world to see.
Sunshine and rainbows,
Mountains and meadows,
Honeysuckle and bees, *zzzzz*
Weeping willow trees.

Look, it's good.

In the beginning,
In the beginning,
God created the world, a world to hear.
Polar bears and arctic fox,
Snowy owls *Whoo, whoo* and musk ox.
Wolves and lemmings,
Whales that sing.

Listen, it's good.

In the beginning,
In the beginning,
God created the world,
 a world to taste.
Oranges *Yummm* and lemons,
Limes and persimmons.
Coconuts and mangoes,
Green avocados.

Taste, it's good.

In the beginning,
In the beginning,
God created the world,
 a world to smell.
Lilacs and raindrops,
Roses and forget-me-nots.
Skunks and stinkbugs *puuu*,
Grandma's hugs.

Smell, it's good.

In the beginning,
In the beginning,
God created the world,
a world to feel.
Wet sand and cool water *splasssh*,
Seashells and sand dollars.
Warm sun and soft breeze,
Sunburned knees!

Feel, it's good.

In the beginning,
In the beginning,
God created the world,
a world to know.
Morning and evening,
Winter and spring,
Summer and fall,
God loves us all.

Know, it's good.
Thank you, God.

In the beginning, God created.
Genesis 1:1